Newbridge Discovery Links®

OUR
West

Lillian Schlissel

Newbridge

A Haights Cross Communications Company

Our West
ISBN: 1-58273-728-2

Program Author: Dr. Brenda Parkes
Content Reviewer: Elisa Kurz, Museum of Western Expansion, St. Louis, MO
Teacher Reviewer: Denise Ott, Olmsted 67, Buffalo, NY

Written by Lillian Schlissel
Editorial and Design Assistance by Curriculum Concepts

Newbridge Educational Publishing
333 East 38th Street, New York, NY 10016
www.newbridgeonline.com

Cover Photograph: Prairies of the West
Table of Contents Photograph: A wagon train

Photo Credits
Cover: Joseph Sohm, ChromoSohm, Inc./CORBIS; Contents page: CORBIS; pages 4-5: Leo L.
Larson/Panoramic Images; page 6: Stock Montage, Inc.; pages 8–9: Denver Public Library Western History
Department; page 11: Bettmann/CORBIS; page 12: Bettmann/CORBIS; page 13: Used by permission,
Utah State Historical Society, all rights reserved, photo no. 10106; pages 14–15: CORBIS; page 15: Stock
Montage, Inc.; page 16: The Granger Collection; page 17: Minnesota Historical Society/CORBIS; pages
18–19: Ozark National Forest Arkansas USA/CORBIS; page 20: Solomon D. Butcher Collection,
Nebraska State Historical Society; page 21: The Kansas State Historical Society Topeka, Kansas; page 22:
Stock Montage, Inc.; page 23: The Granger Collection; page 24: Courtesy Museum of New Mexico Neg
no. 22468; page 25: Courtesy Museum of New Mexico Neg no. 137333; pages 26–27: The Granger
Collection; pages 28–29: Joseph Sohm, Visions of America/CORBIS; page 29: Lawrence Migdale

Maps/Illustrations: Susan Johnston Carlson, page 7;
    Gershom Griffith, page 10; Robert Steimle, page 30

10 9 8 7 6 5 4 3 2

Table of Contents

DREAMS
of a Golden Land

In the early 1840s, the United States was more than 50 years old, and many eastern farmers felt "crowded" by neighbors as close as 12 miles away. They wanted more land. Families in Pennsylvania, Ohio, Indiana, and Illinois had already begun to move west. They heard about "free land" with a milder climate. People said that there was so much food that roasted pigs ran about with knives and forks sticking in them so that you could cut off a slice whenever you were hungry!

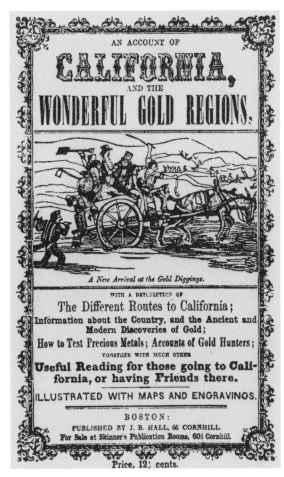

AN ACCOUNT OF

CALIFORNIA,
AND THE
WONDERFUL GOLD REGIONS.

A New Arrival at the Gold Diggings.

WITH A DESCRIPTION OF

The Different Routes to California;

Information about the Country, and the Ancient and
Modern Discoveries of Gold;

How to Test Precious Metals; Accounts of Gold Hunters;

TOGETHER WITH MUCH OTHER

**Useful Reading for those going to Cali-
fornia, or having Friends there.**

ILLUSTRATED WITH MAPS AND ENGRAVINGS.

BOSTON:
PUBLISHED BY J. B. HALL, 66 CORNHILL.
For Sale at Skinner's Publication Rooms, 60½ Cornhill.

Price, 12½ cents.

*Flyers, books, and newspaper articles helped
tell about the wonders and riches that
rewarded those people willing to travel west.*

In 1845, a newspaper article set forth the idea that America was meant to spread from the Atlantic Ocean to the Pacific Ocean. "It is our **manifest destiny**," the author wrote, "to overspread and to possess the whole of the continent. . . ." Easterners liked this idea, and "manifest destiny" became a slogan for **westward expansion**. Within five years, Texas, Oregon, and California were states and the rest of the vast region was United States territory.

It was roughly 2,000 miles from Independence, Missouri, where most wagon trails started, to California. But thousands of Americans were ready for new opportunities. Even more people went west in 1849 after gold was discovered near San Francisco. The news brought people not only from the eastern states, but from Europe, Asia, and South America as well.

Whether the **pioneers** were looking for a new farm or a fortune in gold, in crossing the continent they had to leave family and friends—and anything else that could not fit into a covered wagon.

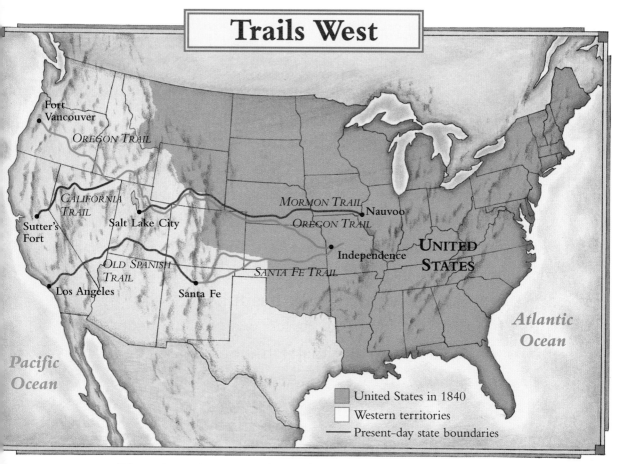

The main trails west are shown above. Between 1840 and 1870 more than 250,000 pioneers took these trails.

A DIFFICULT *Journey*

Pioneers had to find a way to get their wagons over mountains and across rivers and deserts. They had to live outdoors during a journey that often took six months.

To travel overland, a wagon had to be strong enough to carry a family and provisions. It took $600 to $800 to put together a wagon, a team of oxen, and supplies. Food and other provisions could cost hundreds of dollars more, depending on how large a family might be.

A thousand dollars for a loaded wagon was a hefty sum in those days. Beyond that, families needed cash for emergencies along the way. If they took a ferry, they had to pay a toll. When they reached their journey's end, they needed enough money to build a new home and raise new crops. Most **overlanders** sold their farms and furniture back east to raise the money they needed.

Provisions:

1. milk pails
2. grease for wheels
3. oil lamps
4. frying pans
5. rope
6. dishes
7. rifles
8. spinning wheels

Travelers also took flour, salt, bacon, sugar, rice, tea, dried beans, fruit, vinegar, pickles, and tallow for candles.

Hiram Young was an African American blacksmith with a shop in Independence, Missouri, where the **Oregon Trail** started. He became famous for his freight wagons and ox yokes. The wagons had enormous wagon wheels made of wood with iron "belts" stretched around them. No ordinary wagon could withstand the punishing journey. Young received government contracts for wagons to haul freight from Independence to Santa Fe.

The largest wagon, called the **Conestoga wagon**, weighed 3,000 pounds—about as much as an automobile—and could carry another 10,000 pounds when it was fully loaded. It was pulled by teams of horses, mules, or powerful oxen. But even oxen could not pull such a heavy load over the demanding terrain of the Oregon Trail. That is why a new and lighter wagon, called a **prairie schooner**, became popular, especially with pioneers who traveled overland to Oregon.

Prairie schooners had covers that dipped down in the middle. They were about half the size of Conestoga wagons. Mr. Vanderburgh describes how he and his family prepared for their journey in a prairie schooner:

Six children and all those hundreds and hundreds of miles!... I bought three fine teams...one a four-horse team, and three wagons, and canvas to make wagon covers and a tent.... We can take very little food and clothing. We will get new things in Oregon.

John Kelly Vanderburgh

Not all pioneers had the money for fine, new wagons. Many braved the trails in simple farm wagons. When they could, they fitted their old wagons with canvas covers called **bonnets** to shield themselves and their possessions from the sun, rain, and dust on the trail. Some people even walked all the way.

African Americans were part of the westward expansion. Many African Americans left the South and traveled west after the Civil War ended in 1865.

Why do you think handcarts were designed to be pulled by two people?

For example, one group of pioneers was so eager to make their way to Salt Lake City, Utah, that they made the journey with handcarts instead of wagons. They were a religious group called Mormons.

There were six to our cart, Father and Mother pulled it; Rosie (two years old) and Christian (six months old) rode; John (9) and I (6) walked. Sometimes, when it was downhill, they let me ride, too.

Mary Ann Hafen

All pioneers, including children, had to adjust in many ways. Although people tried to be careful, there were accidents. Catherine Ann Sager playfully jumped out of her family's wagon while it was moving and broke her leg. A doctor from another wagon train put her leg into a splint, and for the rest of the trip she either rode in the wagon or walked on crutches. Children who had once gone to school now abandoned their lessons, or continued their studies with just a few books and supplies, learning their lessons and their penmanship in a swaying wagon.

Everyone had to help with chores, especially when it came time to set up camp and prepare a meal. Wood and other fuels were scarce, so children and women gathered twigs, grasses, and something they called "buffalo chips" to build their fires.

Food was cooked out of doors. Women and girls gathered wild berries for pies, and tried to bake bread. The men and boys shot game and fished. Most pioneers managed pretty well, except when it rained and when the wind blew sand into their food.

When night fell on the trails, the wagons formed great circles. The oxen, mules, and horses grazed quietly while the travelers ate and told stories around campfires.

Many families traveled together in groups called **wagon trains**.

Pioneers faced big decisions as they progressed along the trail. Would safe drinking water be found along the way? Which route would be the best way to go? When people chose wrong, they might end up stuck in the mud or face-to-face with an impassable canyon or impossibly rocky path. Or they might find themselves with no choice but to cross a river.

There was no way to get to the place where my father had determined to locate us, but to wade through the tremendous swamps. I knew some of the young men that went along laughed at us girls. . . for holding up what dresses we had to keep them from miring; but we did not think it was funny. We finally waded through and got all our goods.

Martha Ann Morriso

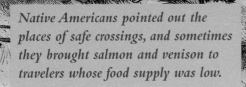

Native Americans pointed out the places of safe crossings, and sometimes they brought salmon and venison to travelers whose food supply was low.

When pioneers came to a shallow river, they would attempt to take their wagons right through. To cross deep rivers, everyone had to unload their possessions onto rafts and float them across while the men swam the oxen and wagons through the water.

Martha Ann Morrison was 13 when she went west. Her family had to leave their wagon on the road and go down the Deschutes River in an open canoe. Then they waded through muddy swamps into the Willamette Valley in Oregon.

As difficult as the Morrison family journey was, they all arrived safely. But then, like all of the pioneers who reached their destinations, they had to face the challenges of building a new life in the West.

MANY DREAMS, *Many Peoples*

One of the first things that settlers had to do was build new homes. In places where timber was plentiful, whole communities turned out to help new families build their log cabins.

But even when there were neighbors nearby to help, there was nothing easy about frontier farming. Since overlanders arrived with only oxen, they had to buy or breed cows, chickens, pigs, and mules. Wells had to be dug to draw water, and the animals had to be fed in all kinds of weather. In some places, like California and Oregon, the weather was usually mild, but some settlers faced blizzards so severe that a trip of 20 yards to the barn could be deadly.

The Shoals family of Nebraska in front of their soddy

The sod wall [of the house] is about 2 feet thick at the ground and slopes off on the outside to about 14 inches at the top. The roof is composed of a ridge pole and rafters of rough split logs on which is laid corn stalks and on top of those are two layers of sod. The roof has a very slight pitch for if it had more, the sod would wash off when there is heavy rain. . . . Some sod houses are mighty comfortable places to go into in cold weather, and it don't take much fire to keep them warm. . . .

Howard Ruede

A Kansas pioneer wrote to the folks back home about his sod house.

Homesteaders in Kansas and Nebraska lived on flat **prairies** where there were no trees. They had to learn to cut bricks of **sod**, squares of earth held together by grass roots, to build their houses.

The tough prairie land had never been plowed, and horses that pulled the plows gave out before the first harvest.

The settlers also discovered that what they had planted back East was not always well-suited to the long winters and harsh climate found in parts of the West. Immigrants brought seeds from Russia for "winter wheat," which sprouted when snow was still on the ground.

Women, especially, worked much harder than they had back East. They raised children, kept house, and fed hired hands. Sometimes they even split logs and branded cattle.

Pioneer families often included many children. Even young children helped with the chores.

To the settlers, the West was an "undiscovered" land, but it was already home to many Native Americans, who hunted herds of buffalo, farmed, and fished. Soon, their way of life was threatened by the arrival of so many new people. As the pioneers built more homes and farmed more land in the West, once-friendly Indians began to resent their new neighbors. Sometimes there were conflicts. Native Americans raided some farms, and the newcomers sometimes raided Native American settlements. Each group hoped to drive the other away from what they considered their land.

The Lakota hunted buffalo and built tipis made of buffalo hide. They were among the people whose way of life was threatened when settlers and railroad construction led to the destruction of the buffalo herds.

Oh, what a fright we all got one morning to hear some white people were coming. Oh, I never can forget it. My poor mother was carrying my little sister on her back and trying to make me run... my aunt overtook us and she said "Let us bury our girls, or we shall all be killed." So our mothers buried me and my cousin, planting sage over our faces to keep the sun from burning them and there we were left all day [until the white people left]. Oh, can anyone imagine my feelings of being buried alive?

Sarah Winnemucca

Sarah Winnemucca's writing helped many people learn about the westward expansion from a Native American point of view.

Sarah Winnemucca, of the Paiute nation, was among the people who feared the strangers coming into their lands. Despite her early fears, Sarah grew up having contact with many different people. She learned English and Spanish and became an interpreter. She married a European American, met a president, and wrote her autobiography.

The settlers who made their homes in the Southwest met people of Spanish descent who had already lived in the area for generations. What would happen to their culture? Now there were more people in California who spoke English than there were people who spoke Spanish. The *Californios* did lose much of

Spanish-speaking families like this one farmed and ranched in the valleys from New Mexico to California.

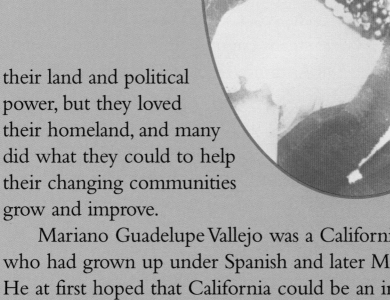

their land and political power, but they loved their homeland, and many did what they could to help their changing communities grow and improve.

Mariano Guadelupe Vallejo was a Californio leader who had grown up under Spanish and later Mexican rule. He at first hoped that California could be an independent nation, but later came to believe that California should become part of the United States. He liked the idea of being part of a democratic nation in which the people elected their own leaders. Vallejo became one of the first state senators when California established its own state government.

Not every newcomer settled on a farm. Men from China were among the immigrants who came to seek their fortunes in the gold fields. Many ended up staying to work on the railroads and took jobs in growing towns and cities.

In time, railroads took up the job of carrying people across America. Workers blasted through mountain ranges and laid tracks across deserts, connecting cattle towns like Abilene, Texas, and Wichita, Kansas. Gold rush towns like Sacramento and San Francisco, California, were easily reached by rails. Great steam engines chugged into old Spanish towns like San Antonio, Texas, and Santa Fe, New Mexico. Salt Lake City, Utah, Phoenix, Arizona, and Denver, Colorado, grew into major urban centers. Seattle, Washington, and Portland, Oregon, thrived in the Northwest. The West kept growing and changing as more new people followed their dreams to this golden land.

San Francisco, California, in 1847

Immigrants from China and other lands became a vital part of life in cities such as San Francisco and Seattle.

OUR *West*

The West has continued to attract people from all over the world who are looking for a new start. Today, California has more people born in other nations than any other state. Texas and Arizona also have large **immigrant** populations. Many of these newcomers arrived from Mexico, but

San Francisco, California, today

there are also Vietnamese, Hmong, Russians, Koreans, Pakistanis, and people from Madagascar, India, and Hong Kong. Each group adds its distinctive mark on western culture and communities. Today, as before, westerners are open to new ideas and new challenges.

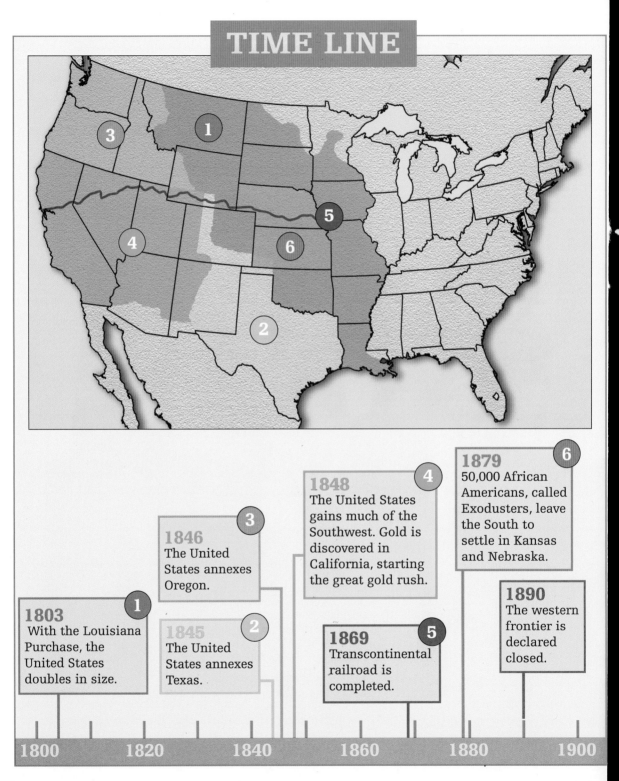

TIME LINE

1803 ① With the Louisiana Purchase, the United States doubles in size.

1845 ② The United States annexes Texas.

1846 ③ The United States annexes Oregon.

1848 ④ The United States gains much of the Southwest. Gold is discovered in California, starting the great gold rush.

1869 ⑤ Transcontinental railroad is completed.

1879 ⑥ 50,000 African Americans, called Exodusters, leave the South to settle in Kansas and Nebraska.

1890 The western frontier is declared closed.

1800   1820   1840   1860   1880   1900

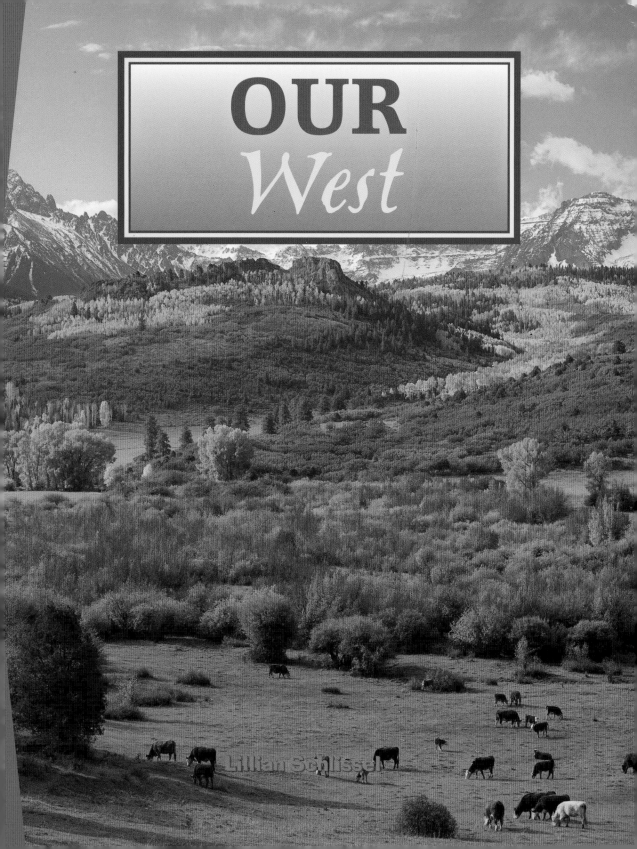

OUR
West

Lillian Schlissel

Glossary

bonnets: the canvas covers of wagons

Conestoga wagon: a heavy wagon with a canvas top that was first built in the Conestoga region of Pennsylvania and used to transport freight

immigrants: people who go to another country and live there permanently

manifest destiny: the idea, which later became a widespread belief, that the United States was fated or divinely intended to reach from sea to sea

Oregon Trail: a route used by pioneers in the mid–1800s stretching northwest from Independence, Missouri, to Oregon

overlanders: people who traveled by land from the East Coast across the continent to the West

pioneers: people who were among the first to settle in a certain territory

prairie: a flat or rolling land of grasses and wildflowers with few or no trees

prairie schooner: a wagon with a canvas top that dipped in the center and often reminded people of ships called schooners; often a simple farm wagon with a bonnet and lighter than a Conestoga wagon

sod: the top layer of soil and the grass attached to it

westward expansion: the growth of the United States westward with the Louisiana Purchase, annexation of Texas, annexation of Oregon, and the addition of a vast region once part of Mexico

Index

Websites

To learn more about the opening of the West, check out

www.isu.edu/~trinmich/Oregontrail.html

www.pbs.org/wgbh/amex/kids/goldrush/index.html

www.pbs.org/opb/oregontrail